Trains

Eurostar

by Julie Murray

2

Dash!
LEVELED READERS
An Imprint of Abdo Zoom • abdobooks.com

Dash!
LEVELED READERS

2

Level 1 – Beginning
Short and simple sentences with familiar words or patterns for children who are beginning to understand how letters and sounds go together.

Level 2 – Emerging
Longer words and sentences with more complex language patterns for readers who are practicing common words and letter sounds.

Level 3 – Transitional
More developed language and vocabulary for readers who are becoming more independent.

THIS BOOK CONTAINS RECYCLED MATERIALS

abdobooks.com

Published by Abdo Zoom, a division of ABDO, PO Box 398166, Minneapolis, Minnesota 55439. Copyright © 2022 by Abdo Consulting Group, Inc. International copyrights reserved in all countries. No part of this book may be reproduced in any form without written permission from the publisher. Dash!™ is a trademark and logo of Abdo Zoom.

Printed in the United States of America, North Mankato, Minnesota.
102021
012022

Photo Credits: Getty Images, iStock, Shutterstock, ©Rcsprinter123 p.6 / CC BY 3.0
Production Contributors: Kenny Abdo, Jennie Forsberg, Grace Hansen, John Hansen
Design Contributors: Candice Keimig, Neil Klinepier, Victoria Bates

Library of Congress Control Number: 2021940202

Publisher's Cataloging in Publication Data

Names: Murray, Julie, author.
Title: Eurostar / by Julie Murray
Description: Minneapolis, Minnesota : Abdo Zoom, 2022 I Series: Trains I Includes online resources and index.
Identifiers: ISBN 9781098226725 (lib. bdg.) I ISBN 9781644947241 (pbk.) I ISBN 9781098227562 (ebook) I ISBN 9781098227982 (Read-to-Me ebook)
Subjects: LCSH: Eurostar (Express train)--Juvenile literature. I Railroads--Juvenile literature. I Express trains--Juvenile literature. I Transportation--Juvenile literature. I Railroad travel--Juvenile literature.
Classification: DDC 388.42--dc23

Table of Contents

Eurostar

Eurostar is a high-speed train service. It first opened in 1994.

It links **Great Britain** to France, Belgium, and the Netherlands.

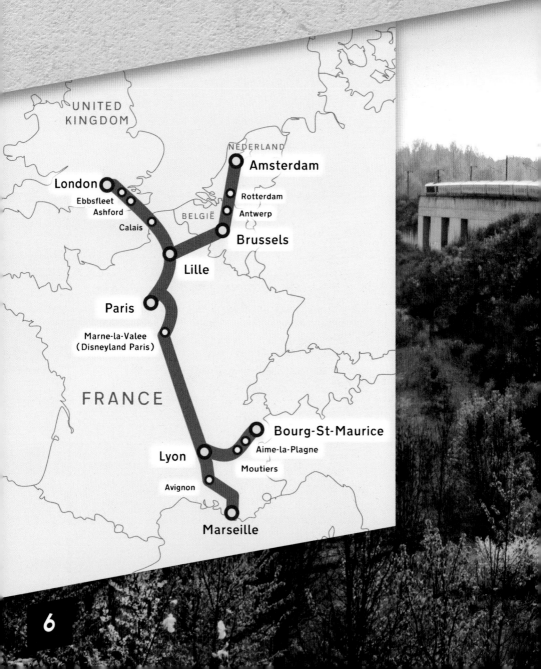

Nearly 30 trains run on the **system**. Some can hold 900 passengers.

The trains can go fast.
The high-speed **line** can
go 200 miles per hour
(320 kph).

The trains run above and below ground. A part of Eurostar runs under the **English Channel**.

Channel Tunnel

QUIZZ DU

EUROSTAR™

TUNNEL

›Londres

The Channel Tunnel, or Chunnel, is an undersea tunnel! It connects **Great Britain** to the European mainland. The Chunnel is 31.5 miles long.

45 km

,45 km
ngueur de chaque tunnel

The Chunnel sits 246 feet (75 m) below **sea level** at its deepest point.

The train slows to 100 mph
(161 kph) in the Chunnel
for safety. Around 60,000
people ride each day.

The train doesn't just carry passengers. Cars and motorcycles can ride aboard too!

More Facts

- Eurostar trains are a quarter mile long (402 m). Workers ride bikes from one end of the train to the other.

- More than 200 million people have ridden the Eurostar since it opened.

- Eurostar has its own robot. Her name is Pepper. She speaks English and French.

Glossary

English Channel – an extension of the Atlantic Ocean between England and France.

Great Britain – the main island of the United Kingdom located off the coast of France. It includes England, Scotland, and Wales.

line – one of the many different lines, or railway, in a train system. Lines can be different sizes and serve different people. Some lines allow trains to move faster than others.

sea level – the surface level of the sea, halfway between high and low tide. It is used as the starting point for measuring elevations and depths.

system – a group of parts that work together as a whole.

Index

Online Resources

Booklinks
NONFICTION NETWORK
FREE! ONLINE NONFICTION RESOURCES

To learn more about Eurostar, please visit **abdobooklinks.com** or scan this QR code. These links are routinely monitored and updated to provide the most current information available.